Speak English, You're in America

Carolina Abreu

Speak English, You're in America
Copyright © 2021 Carolina Abreu
ISBN-13: 978-0-578-73832-1

Cover Art: Waldo Baez Reyes
Editor: Roxana Calderón

Instagram: @ughvolution
Website: ughvolution.com
Email: info@ughvolution.com

IT IS NEVER TOO LATE
TO NURTURE OURSELVES
AND HEAL THE PARTS OF
US THAT KEEP US FROM
BECOMING WHO WE ARE.

PREFACE

August 17th, 2002.

I opened my eyes and stared up at the ceiling fan that was barely hanging on by a couple of cables for the last time. It's funny how you start to miss the things that are right in front of you once you realize you may never see them again. Same thing happens with people. I had no idea how long the fan would stay connected to the ceiling the same way I had no idea how long I would stay connected to my land. *Would every passing day fade away a chunk of my memory?* I wondered and immediately shrugged it off. I had more immediate things to worry about like saying goodbye to Mamá and the rest of my family who had been taking care of me and my sister for the last two years.

I was unable to come up with an idea of what New York would be like. Even when I first arrived, I didn't know what to make of it. I could only describe it as different.

Back home, I always felt like I was exactly where I was supposed to be. I belonged to the Dominican Republic, and it belonged to me. In New York, it was difficult to belong to all the changes, the seasons, and the language.

I felt cold inside, no matter the temperature.

Belonging feels like warmth.

I attempted to create separation, as if there was a me that only belonged in the Dominican Republic and another me who desperately tried to fit in America. I attempted to choose sides and when it all felt impossible, I told myself I didn't deserve any of it. I alone created more distance inside of me than the 2,470 km that separates New York from the Dominican Republic.

One day, when I heard the words *"Speak English, you're in America,"* said to me and I was certain that I'd never know the feeling of belonging again. I took charge of making sure I didn't so that no one else had the power to do that for me again.

I chose to never stay in relationships, friendships, majors in school or places. There was no reason to if I didn't belong to any of it.

That was then.

Today, I know that I do belong. I belong here in the United States. I belong back home in the Dominican Republic. I belong in my relationships. I belong in my friendships. I belong in my family.

I belong in English.

I belong in Spanish.

TABLE OF CONTENTS

Belonging

The best thing about
being from two places
is that you don't have to
commit to either.

You take what you want
from each
and leave the rest
up to not belonging.

Does it Count?

I imagined
my first kiss
a million times
before it happened.

I day-dreamed for hours on end
that it would come from David,
my 5th grade crush
and one of the most
popular kids in my grade.

The way his braces worked hard
to close the gap between his teeth
and his shirt hung lifeless
over his scrawny body,
made me go back and forth
between scenarios.

What would I do when
he finally came over to
profess his undying love?

I thought of him kissing me

while the rest of the kids stood

around us at recess,

hiding us from the nuns,

filling the air with gasps and *"aww!"*

I've always been a dreamer.

Instead,

it came from my cousin,

whom as I said one last goodbye

to my family before leaving to the United States,

planted one on me and said:

«Toma, para que no te vayas a besar

con un negro de allá».

Memories

We were never conventional.

It felt normal,

the screaming

as I woke up on the couch

from an afternoon nap.

The same warm breeze

that laid me to sleep

still grazing my legs.

The words

"Pack your things we are leaving."

caressed my cheeks

as I thought of ways to pack my dad.

He was mine

and I, his

even though he let us go each time.

"I'll pick you up next week."

I always knew he would.

                    Memories...

of when it finally felt old.

I no longer felt afraid

of leaving something behind.

Home

I always wanted them to buy a house.

People that live in houses, *stay*.

I believed it meant commitment

to a place,

to each other,

to love.

Marriage alone

would not make them stay.

Their commitment

was only loyal to change

and to the lack of itself.

Flying Objects

This isn't a story about Aliens. This is a story about the
time my cousin, my uncle and I sat in our terrace on a
humid day, singing: *"Juana, Juana, pélame la banana. Si no me
la pelas, me la pela tu hermana!"* at the top of our lungs.

My grandma, *Mamá* who had been ironing everyone's
clothes for hours had told us to stop a few times. Finally
reaching the end of her patience, she grabbed the bottle of
ironing starch and with precise aim, lunged it at me. A part
of me was expecting something similar, so I reacted by
raising my arm and stopping the bottle with my wrist. I
still feel my wrist throb every time I see a bottle of ironing
starch.

As the bottle made its way to me, my cousin and uncle had
time to react, and they had started their running exit from
anywhere near my grandmother's perimeter. This
prompted *Mamá* to send her *chancleta* flying towards my
cousin getting her in the back of the head and grabbing the
broomstick and smacking *Guelo* right on his back.

Needless to say, we then all made the decision to stop
singing and instead watch TV in the bedroom. A few
minutes later, mama walks in and asks:

"¿Tienen hambre?"

Mama's Kitchen

In *Mamá*'s kitchen,
nothing had a single use.
The stove roasted the most
delicious *pernil* during Christmas time,
and also dried up my school uniform
on brisk mornings
when I ran late to school.

The kitchen table
is where she served us
every single one of our meals
and where my mom, *tías*, and herself
sat around when la *salonera* came over
once a week.

The *callejón* is where she would
hang our clothes to dry
and later, where she would line up
my cousins and I
to bathe us with the hose.
In her kitchen
is where she usually tries to hide
every time we have to say goodbye

before we head back to the states
but we always know where to find her,
except for the last time.

I headed to the kitchen
tears already making my cheeks warm,
hating the fact that I had to say goodbye
again, and still not being used to it.

She wasn't there.

This time,
she locked herself in the bathroom
which makes sense because
we haven't made any memories there.

We didn't get to say goodbye the last time I left.
What I have left now,
is the hope that I'll get to hug her
in her kitchen again.

Pan de maíz

Abuela's recipe
will never be done
the way she does it.

It doesn't matter
how many times
she writes it down for me,
I'll always know
it won't be the same
because I don't have her soft hands.

Soft hands to go
with her soft heart,
even though life
has been hard on her.

I imagine that when
she lost her love
the universe stopped.

And as if to apologize to her
it gathered all the love
and strength from all corners

of the world and placed them
inside of her.

How lucky am I?

To know I'll always have
a place,
a person,
a heart,
a memory
and hands,
so soft to lay on
and gather my own strength
when life is hard on me.

I can't help but wonder,
who did that for her?

Heladero

Shoes were only a choice.

Rain or shine,

we had no limits,

our bodies sticky with sweat

shining under the hot sun.

The world was our playground.

¡Ding, ding, ding!

¡Heladero!

We looked around in awe,

as if this wasn't our everyday routine.

Who could run the fastest

to yell for the coins that

already awaited us?

There was no loser

as our mouths dripped

with different flavors

under the mango tree.

I couldn't help but wonder
if the *heladero* ever had a chance
to run for change himself
back when he was my age.

Forgotten

There's a big difference between living in your homeland and going to visit it. When you live in your homeland you know the ins and outs of it, you are up to date with new landmarks and which neighbors are still in the neighborhood. When you go visit, you are constantly trying to remember names and locations and things that no longer are, my late dog Sparkly reminded me of that difference.

It was the first time I went back home after moving to America. A few years had gone by and the closer I got to *Mamá's* house, the more excited I grew. I could barely contain myself. I pictured getting out of the car and my dog running ahead of everyone to come say hello and jump into my arms. Instead, my mom, sister, dad and I stood outside waiting for my grandma to find her keys to let us in and my dog was nowhere in sight.

We finally got inside, hugged, and kissed everyone hello when out of the corner of my eye I saw my dog wearily walking towards us and barking. I started walking towards him, arms wide open and on my way to kneel down when I noticed my dog's snarl; loud enough to stop me in my tracks and approach the situation differently. I held my arm out

while bending down slowly to allow Sparkly to sniff my
scent and remember me so that we could start over. He
responded by growling louder and showing more teeth.

I decided to give him some time. I waited the rest of my
vacation. I waited a few years until I returned and tried
again, and I waited until Sparkly was no longer with us to
accept that he had forgotten me. It was then that I started
to wonder who else would forget me and what other
memories would fade away forever?

Different

Reborn in foreign land,

neighbors are now strangers,

seasons change,

and people care about what language

your thoughts are in.

The leaves come and go,

traffic is always there.

Your name becomes

unfamiliar to yourself.

You stop correcting them,

until you are old enough to realize

it does matter what they call you.

Your dream now has a nationality,

and you start to rush

even if you have no clue

where you are going.

You feel guilty

because it starts to feel like home...

Dreams

"What language do you dream in?"

Mis sueños no tienen lengua.

Instead,

ask me what my dreams are

and I will welcome you into them.

They speak to all

and you could hear them too,

if you weren't so focused on its tongue.

Middle School

I was terrified to start middle school in the United States. I was also slightly excited. A week before I started, I would sit and imagine what it would be like. In my mind, it looked exactly like the movies. Rows of lockers, where kids stopped to chat between classes, cool projects being lugged around for science class and delicious lunch served in a big cafeteria where everybody was friends.

The reality was a bit different. I remember the first fight between two students that I witnessed. I was walking down the hallway with friends heading from one class to the next, when I heard the *"ooohs!"* and the *"ohs!"* and saw students all running towards the same place. I looked over to one of my friends and asked what was going on to which she replied: *"It's a fight, come on!"* and started running towards it.

At the time, I couldn't understand the concept of a fight inside of the school hallways. Back home in school, we were constantly watched by the nuns and priests, and kids knew not to even consider stepping out of line like that. After a few weeks, hallway fights became a normal part of my day-to-day and I knew that once I heard the yelling and saw the people running to move out of the way and continue going about my day.

The bullying started a few months later for me. I was in gym class and a girl from an older grade came up to me and asked:

"Where are your shoes from, Payless?"

At the time, I didn't register the sarcasm and I excitedly replied with a smile and one of the English words I felt confident enough to say out loud:

"Yes!"

It wasn't the reply she was expecting and she took it as "disrespect" which gained me months of bullying and threats until one day, she along with 5 of her friends caught me walking down the hallway alone as we switched classes, surrounded me and beat me up.

As I stood surrounded by 6 girls and an overexcited crowd who were yelling things at me I was too scared to understand, I could hear my sister's voice as she gave me tips to survive school in America:

"If a group of people try to jump you, just focus all your energy on one of them and fight as hard as you can. Someone will stop them."

I did just that until I felt the hands of a much older teacher break up the fight, pick me up, take me into her empty classroom and close the door behind her.

"Are you okay?" she asked.

"Yes." I replied.

Speak English, You're in America

It was my second or third winter in America
and I'd never been slapped in the face by
anything as cold as her words.

The embarrassment wrapped around me
like a hot blanket under the sun
and I wasn't sure if I should stick out
a limb or two so that I wouldn't burn.

Ms. Herrington's blue eyes
pierced through me,
opening a hole in my chest
that exposed innocence as it left my body
and the anger that began to consume me.

I froze and allowed this storm to wreak havoc
inside of me.
I allowed it to move all the pieces
that made up who I was and change me;
make me hard.

The sound of the bell snapped me back
into reality and I knew nothing was the same.

I had just learned how to harbor anger inside of me.

I collected my things and stuffed them into my bag.

I started to walk out of the room but not without

first looking up at my monster.

Her eyes, which before looked like ice,

now resembled the sky;

soft and almost apologetic poetic in a way.

Her lips...

Her lips remained tightly sealed,

revealing the wrinkles that guarded her mouth

 and prevented softer words from making their way to me.

My eyes, the color of coconuts mixed with sand

mustered up all of the sun that they could,

not to tan or warm, but to burn

as I exited the room.

The revolution had just begun.

Dementia

He didn't forget me;

he forgot how to love me,

which is only fair because in the midst

of me learning all the anger that I know today,

I forgot how to love him.

The difference is,

one of us still has the ability to learn.

He forgot the joy of being alive

while teaching me the importance

of being present.

He forgot about boundaries,

which in the right context

I'd like to forget about too,

so that I no longer force myself

to live within the limits of my own.

The worst thing is,

there is no one to blame.

Sometimes I wish he was dead,

only because there is nothing worse

than mourning someone while they're still alive.

I've locked away the memories
in the deepest parts of my being,
so that they no longer force me
to think about the beautiful times.
I remember when we used to ride in his car singing
The Beatles at the top of our lungs:

*"Close your eyes and I'll kiss you
Tomorrow I'll miss you."*

Tomorrow I will miss you!

Yet, I can't seem to let go of today.
How dare life take you away from me,
And leave you here at the same time
as if to mock me?

Dangling the fact that I can see you
but I can't see you.
Will you ever see me?
All I can do is hope that tomorrow
will be enough.
I just can't do today
but tomorrow, I will miss you.

My mother and I bond

1. How fast we can run away when we see a *voladora*

2. Our inability to stop picking food from the pots even though "We're full."

3. Sarcasm

4. Using different voices to trick my dad on the phone when he calls because it's easier to be funny than to admit we miss him and that it hurts

5. Getting mad at each other before accepting we are hurt

6. Fighting when we are together, calling each other every day when we are apart

7. Making jokes when things get too serious

8. Unconditional support

9. Never admitting we are wrong

10. Sprinting from the elevator to the door to use the bathroom first every time we get home

Stage 4

It was eating her alive,
the cancer.
It was eating me alive,
the anger.

Not one of us said a thing.
If pretending to be okay was the cure,
there would have been nothing to heal.

If we never got the call,
we would've never known
that she was stage 4.

Her life was a stage.
She woke up every day
and lived through the script
she had come up with
just the night before;
written on her pillow,
her tears were the ink.

I am in awe of her presence,
her body

tells a story of time.

The pages wrinkle

as she goes through life.

When I look at my mother,

I always start with her eyes

the creases at the corners

invite me to experience

her every smile.

Her hair,

grey and white

reminds me that time

cannot be stopped.

Each strand holds a

piece of knowledge,

like seeds that fall onto

the palms of my hands,

as I run my fingers through.

I will plant them.

In my heart

I will water them

with memories

every time I think about
what my mother had to go
through just to remain alive.

The flowers that bloom
will be the tickets to the
place we'll both land on
as soon as we are done
accepting what the other is.

I am my mother's daughter,
strong-minded
but even more, soft-hearted.

She,
her mother's daughter,
who would slap away
any hand that tried to
run their fingers through
her hair.

Attention

I used to cut myself.
The wounds,
never deep enough
for the pain to bleed
completely out.

Ironically, I hid them,
pretending I didn't want
to be noticed.

It made me feel important.
The thought that
if someone found out,
they would have cared
and asked what was wrong.

That for that moment,
I'd become the center of attention
and possibly told it would be okay
and that I was safe.

But I hid them and then,
I learned to fight through the darkness.

Accent

My Dominican accent
gets made fun of,
but it is mine.

My American accent
tells them
I don't belong.

When you read this,
you can't tell if I wrote it
in Dominican
or American.

What is there left
other than my voice
and my existence?

Dementia II

I never got to fully know you.
I loved the version of you
I knew as a child.

Baby powder all over the floor,
your legs spread wide for me
to slide under until the wall
stopped me.

Maps and last-minute destinations,
buying nuts and fruits from
every vendor along the way.
Loud music & singalongs
with made up English words.

Then, this version of you
came sweeping through.
What happened to the before?
What happened to what was
supposed to be?
We are stuck in this in-between.
All I have are these old articles
and stories that feel too unfamiliar.

I want to know more,

I want to know who you wanted to be,

And did you always plan for me?

What stories about

my childhood

would be your favorite to tell?

Did you ever notice when

I started to behave badly,

just to get your attention?

Did it work?

I want to know less.

I want to erase the stories

that are told from the perspective

of everyone else's stories.

I want to erase the stories

of your selfishness and your

abandonment.

I want to know you.

You. And no one else.

Lyrics

When we were younger,

my sisters and I

would sprint over to my father's car,

yelling and shoving each other,

demanding our spots.

As soon as we got inside,

we'd rummage through his CDs,

picking at random

and making up words

as we sang along.

It never seemed important

to make an effort to learn

the real English words;

when would I ever need them?

Now,

in America,

it mattered less which seat

I got in the car

and more that I remembered

to bring my manilla folder

in which I carried

printed out lyrics
of the most current songs on the radio.

My focus shifted from
singing for fun
to desperately needing
to understand and memorize each lyric;
to make sense of this foreign language
that offered me everything
and nothing at all.

Screaming

I prefer to scream on paper.

I scream so loud

my pen bleeds

until it doesn't hurt anymore.

Sometimes,

I scream in poetry,

making my pain rhyme.

Other times

I let the noise guide my hand

until it numbs everything.

I scream in Spanish

when it's about love,

you know,

to make it romantic

and sometimes,

the page remains blank,

when even I can't recognize

what it is that I am screaming about.

Permission to Love

I like to say that the first piece I ever wrote was a letter to my mother asking her to allow me to have a boyfriend at 15- years-old. In it, I professed how ready I felt to be allowed to date, how much it would mean to me and how great of a guy my soon to be boyfriend at the time was.

I have never been good at expressing my feelings or desires out loud. It always takes time and a bit of writing for me to land where I'm going. At such a young age, letters were my main form of communication. I would write endless letters that I never sent and some that I did. With this letter, I thought for sure I would get through to my mother. Before I left for school the morning after I wrote it, I put it inside of my own sock drawer and when I arrived at school, I called my house from my pink Razor phone and said:

"I left you something in my sock drawer, can you go get it?" and hung up the phone.

I went through my day as best as I could. I forced myself to not think about it. I went to Volleyball practice, there it was easy to forget, and I braced myself for the moment I walked through our apartment door.

At first my mom acted normal, so I did too and after dinner she sat me down and broke down the news that although it was a nice letter, I was not old enough to have a boyfriend and she didn't want me talking to this boy at school, after-school or anywhere else.

I felt sad, but I was as in love as a 15-year-old could be and instead of giving up, I devised a plan (more like thousands of them) to sneak around and still be able to date the guy I liked so much. After a few months, my mother inevitably found out and gave in. She was the strictest she'd ever been about anything else, but by that time I was already an expert at sneaking around. We dated for 3 of the most significant years of my teens.

This is how the story of my first real heartbreak started. Sometimes I still wonder if I had listened to my mother, could I have saved myself from experiencing pain until I was "older" or "more mature," and would that have made a difference in how I approached love for many years after?

Self-Hatred

A life-long
mime act.

A body
to show men
they don't matter
to me.

Acting out
ways to hate me.
Shutting down
any chance
of being loved.

Building
an invisible box,
waiting
to be freed.

Pretending to
be happy,
to smile,
to be open.

Only needing

to step out

and be seen.

Hero

I used to wonder
what love would be like
without you.
I can't recall how
it happened,
we never cared
much about details.

I built a home
out of songs
and seasons.
If you were to
come back,
there'd be a place
for you to rest.

With you,
I loved the sound
of firetrucks.
I loved picturing you
inside on your way
to being a hero.

Without you,

I despised the

sounds of firetrucks,

I pictured you inside,

on your way to being

someone else's hero.

Damage

I wasn't ready for you.

I was always ready to let go.

Somehow,
self-induced pain
seemed to touch me
in softer ways.

The damage is done
and the only thing I can do is
use the wreckage

       to love better,
        to love stronger.

To never hurt another,
the way that I hurt you.

Stranger Again

The second time I met you
felt less special.
You were already worn down
and beaten by unrequited love.

You reminded me of me
when you first left.
Revenge is never as sweet
as when imagined.

You apologized,
I can't remember exactly for what
and to be honest,
in that moment it didn't matter.

We somehow picked up
further than we left off,
as if 5 years of being strangers
meant nothing at all.

You showed me off
to all your friends
and they would look at me and say:

"Isn't she?"
Yes, yes, I am
or maybe no,
I'm not.

Every time I looked at you
I saw her
and to be unfair,
it was probably all in my brain,
but you couldn't make it right
and all we had left
was to let go.

We gave each other
the chance to love another,
so that we both could see
what we knew all along,
We are perfectly capable of loving
just not when it comes to each other.

Waldenbuch, Germany

Leaving was never
meant to be permanent.

I left because
a part of me needed
to know that,
given the opportunity,
coming back was
a choice I would make.

The need to
look at things
from a yearning point of view
took over.

As my eyes met
newer possibilities
I knew my heart
would long for the familiar.

My insides needed to feel
what returning home felt like
walking into a place

that receives you
with open arms.

I needed to be looked at
the way those who have
never left look at you
when they realize
they too,
have a choice to leave.

Had I never left,
it would have never
been my decision
to come back
and stay.

It Killed Us

My body is the only thing
keeping my soul
from spilling out
and polluting all the
grounds of your existence.

Let it consume you.

I no longer care to hide
the bad behind the good,
the ugly behind the pretty,
or the inexplicable behind
the sweet.

Let the parts of me that
don't make sense
roam free
and then lay in bed
next to your monsters.

Let it consume you
or let it kill us.

Done Before We Started

The screws on my sunglasses were loose,

you said you'd fix them.

You had all the tools-

and then we fell apart.

You always loved making

promises you couldn't keep,

more than you hated

the disappointment in me.

You said you'd fix the sink but,

we drowned in our past sorrows.

We never got to put frames

around our pictures,

it made them too permanent,

for you.

My dresser never made it into the room,

there wasn't enough room for me,

and your ghosts.

And then, we fell apart.

Mango

They say eyes are the windows to the soul

and I should have known

eyes so blue could've never held

my Caribbean soul close.

Still, I tried.

I remember when I used to pick

at the mango tree outside *Mamá's* house,

the struggle was worth it,

because after a few tries

I'd have the juiciest of fruits in my hands.

I treated you like a mango.

I tried to reach you,

threw my love,

and sometimes my shoes.

Compromised myself;

you pretended to fall.

I tried to peel away

your exterior layer

and I should've known,

you weren't ripe
mostly because you
didn't want to be.

Like a stubborn mango
you wanted to go back to the tree,
not knowing that forcing your way back
to the same place you came from
would only leave you to rot.

And I should've known,
that some mangos just don't want
to be sprinkled with salt or with love
they just want to be left alone,
so that they can then out of nowhere,
trip you and blame you for their dark spots.

I should've known,
it never mattered how much
I wanted that mango
that mango had chosen
to not get caught
from the moment I laid my eyes on it.

Weak

Falling in love with me.

meant falling out of love with you.

I had to trade baring my body,

with baring my soul.

"You are too intense."

He said.

"You are too weak."

She replied.

Reflection

You were my wounds.

You were my fear of
abandonment,
my anger,
my inability to trust.

My incessant need
for attention,
my fear,
my judgment,
my shame.

You were my wounds,
nothing else.

That is all you will ever be.

La taza

My cup in New York
doesn't speak the same language
que mi taza en la República Dominicana.

It no longer tells me my future,
Instead, it speaks oat milk
and it is no longer sweet.

I lost myself
somewhere between
Dominican coffee
y el espresso Americano.

I told myself I would give it up.
Maybe if I committed to no longer
putting the poison in me,
I'd feel better about the things I left behind.

Art

A painter will paint you
a picture of the future
in shades of pink and love.

A musician will put their hands
on your body
as if they were playing
a masterpiece.

A poet will speak to you
in rhymes while laying
on a paper of bliss.

They will create for you
a story that seems impossible
to believe
and when you do,
they'll tell you
it wasn't meant for you
but for their make-believe worlds,
you were but the muse.

They will then leave,

to live in their fantasy world
and return each time their story
starts to become dull.

The day you are no longer there,
they will write, sing and paint
about sorrow,
lost love
and pain.

All that will be left is art.

Fleeting Interest

You are everything

I want to run away from,

but you feel like home.

Not the trauma filled four

walls that I escape to,

but the fantasized.

And still, I run.

Letter to the Moon

For all the nights
I spent awake
staring at you.

Scared,
worried.

Hoping your light
would take my
dark away.

You saw me
when no one else did,
with the same light
you saw those that
were miles away.

Did you ever deliver
my messages to them?

Sometimes you
woke me up
from a night I could

finally sleep,
I resented you then,
though all you wanted
was to make sure
I knew somebody
was there.

Last Goodbye

What kind of love were you?
The last time I fell asleep on you
I knew it had to be just that.

I hadn't slept in months,
your chest was the pillow
and the comfort blanket.
The known and the unknown.

I wanted to be anywhere else
but my tired soul begged
me to stay.

To enjoy you one more time
knowing that I could close my eyes
and be okay.

It then begged me to collect my things,
to take my dreams and leave you behind
with our sheets, our photographs
and the voids I could not fill.

Forgiveness

Some say that
they can forgive
but not forget,
but in order
for me to forgive you
I had to forget.

I had to forget
what it was like
to feel joy
at the thought of
dancing on your grave.

I had to forget
the need for revenge,
to make you feel
a fraction of what
you put me through.

I had to forget the
practiced words.
The things I would
say to you,

If ever I was walking
down the street
and ran into you.

I had to forget
what it felt like
to walk around
with the infected
wounds you left.

To forgive you,
I had to forget.

Curious

When you said goodbye
I cried uncontrollably,
not because I was sad to lose you
but because I knew it would be the last time
I'd be hurt by you.

I realized then,
It wasn't love,
It wasn't like;
It wasn't just lust,
but curiosity too.

"La curiosidad mató al gato,"
and curiosity killed
every inch of us.

Reminder

I'm writing to remind
you of what you did,
as it still comes up for me
and I wouldn't want you to forget.

There's a chance
that if you had apologized,
I would have forgiven you.

We'll never know.

As a reminder,
I don't want to know...

White Men Break Hearts Too

I was always told

to never love a Dominican man.

Instead, I was always encouraged

to find a nice *blanquito;*

those would never cheat,

as if cheating is the only way

a woman can be broken.

The irony of the request

always confused me.

The women in my family

birthed and raised

the same men

they told me to stay away from.

I wondered what it took

to learn that somehow

white means better,

and that white means

trustworthiness.

What led them to believe

that a white woman

could raise her white kids
better than they could raise
their brown kids?

What made them stay
with men that hurt them
so bad,
they had to warn their daughters
to not make the same mistakes?

What made them give up
on their own sons?
And instead of holding them accountable,
it became up to us
to not fall into the trap
they created.

Still,
I listened to them
and what I learned is:
white men break hearts too.

Pleasure

I spent many nights
afraid in the dark,
wondering how
such a magical feeling
can be so wrong.

If this is what hell
tastes like,
pour me a cup of fire,
I will burn from
the inside out.

How could I demand
the ways a man
touches my body,
when touching
 my own was a sin?

Touching my body
was my first shot at love,
and only I can love myself
the way that I do.

My hands,
full of my breasts.

My eyes,
full of the sight of
my own curves.

And my spirit
full of desire.

Settling

The pandemic made me
feel trapped,
and I thought of you
and your fragile heart.
I wondered if you were
following the doctor's rules.

You never did.

Were you scared?
Even with your heart at-risk
I never saw you be scared.

I was afraid back then,
of your small town
and how big forever is.

I was afraid of Sundays
and football
and jerseys
and the lack of the outdoors.

I was afraid of people

and the dullness of

conversations

with no destination,

in the same bars.

I was afraid of settling,

for a job,

a neighborhood,

a house,

and love.

I was afraid I would do

the exact thing I did.

I knew it would break you.

I thought about your heart then too...

Microaggressions

1. "You don't look Dominican"
2. "Are you mixed with anything else?"
3. "You speak English like a white girl"
4. "You're Dominican, aren't you supposed to know how to cook?"
5. "You're Dominican, aren't you supposed to know how to dance?"
6. "What language do you dream in?"
7. "I keep forgetting how to pronounce your name, I'll just call you _____"

Repeat After Me

My name is not Dominican enough,

you can find it in not one

but two American states.

"It's Caroleeeena."

"No, not like the state."

"Yes, it's spelled the same."

I've been asked,

"Isn't it easier to just say CaroLIEna?"

but no, it is not easier for me to surrender

to my American-ness

when I feel like I am constantly reminded

of my lack of Dominican-ness.

Avoidance

Hello mirror!

How I have been avoiding you.

When I was a child

I had the perfect excuse,

I wasn't tall enough to reach you,

you didn't exist.

Life was easy back then,

I lived blissfully in my oblivion

but as I grew taller

so did the expectations.

I saw myself cry for the first time

and my emotions now

had a face I didn't recognize

but I knew it was mine.

I took responsibility

for every single feeling,

every single thought

even the ones that weren't mine

and as I grew more confused,

the taller I got.

Now I could see more of myself.

The more I saw
the less I loved the shell that I was in,
I lost control,
I let her go.

She took so many beatings,
she came back
when she couldn't take any more.

I let her in with open arms,
I told her everything would be alright
even though I had no idea how.

I let her rest,
I let her cry,
now here we are,
standing in front of you.

Generational Traumas

Dear Latinas,

let's forgive our mothers.

Let's go back to admiring them

and loving them

the way we did

before we told them

we were ready to

fall in love,

and they became

hard and strict.

When at the same time,

their heart jumped

and remembered every single

heartbreak they experienced

and tried to protect us from

by telling us

"¡Tú ni te sabes lavar el culo bien!"

Let's forgive them

because that was their way of warning us

of the inevitable pain to come.

They already felt it for us.

Let's forgive them,
even though when we came
home crying instead of
holding us, they'd yell
"¡Por estar puteando te pasa!"
and we felt so small.

Dear Latinas, let's forgive our
mothers so that they can then
forgive themselves too.

Papi

I like to sit and imagine
what my father was like
before I got to call him
Papi.

I make up scenarios in my head
of what he made people feel
when he first walked into
a room.

When I eat his favorite foods,
I try to feel what he felt
and when I hear Elvis play on the radio,
I let it travel inside my ears
and head straight to my heart,
the way he still does.

I didn't know him then
and I barely know him now
but still,
I imagine.

Rama de limón

I grew up on a dead-end street in Santo Domingo surrounded by my cousins and a lot of kids from our neighborhood. After school, we would head home, eat, do homework and head outside to play until dinner time. We would spend hours running up and down the street, playing hide and seek, roller blading, riding our scooters and doing whatever thing came to our mind.

Towards the evening, we usually all ended up hanging out right outside of *Mamá's* apartment, sitting on the back of our neighbor's pick-up truck or near it making jokes, laughing, and talking. Time never seemed to be enough. It didn't matter how long we hung out for, we never got tired which meant we were never ready to go back inside.

Mamá would always send my uncle outside to yell out our names and tell us to go inside for dinner. We'd always say we'd be right there and continued with whatever we were doing. Sometimes *Mamá* would send my uncle out twice or a neighbor that might have been leaving at the same time, but the third time was always her, holding a small tree branch, usually lemon because that's the itchy one when slapped against skin.

We never knew she was coming until she'd reach the first unsuspecting one of us, who would usually jump and yelp announcing to the rest of us that it was time to make a run for it. We'd disperse quickly, running towards the house as she ran after us, herding us with the power of the lemon tree branch. Once we were all inside, she'd help us wash our hands for dinner by pouring water from the water and bleach tank, she kept in the back of the kitchen because she didn't trust our plumbing system.

Dinner was always already served for us.

Mamá's Food

The phrase 'I love you"
can be spoken in over
6,000 languages.

You can scream it,
sing it,
write it
or whisper it.

You can tattoo it
on yourself,
write it on paper
or perhaps,
paint it.

You can show it
with one look,
one touch,
one act of kindness.

You can serve it on a plate,
and that's how I learned it best,
at mama's house,

where love is served warm,
full of flavor
and with *fritos* on the side.

Beauty

How do you define it?
Is it by the standards of men?

The way you feel around the ones
that let everything out as they cum,
but retreat at the thought of letting out
what is really inside?

Or by the catcalls you get
as you walk down the street
and they stare at your behind
demanding that you smile?

The same men go home
to their 13-year-old girls.
The girls that are still hopeful
and innocently in love
with their fathers.

The ones that raised them to be tough
in a world built on their desires.

And what about the ones that raised you?

They tell you:

> You should be this,
> you should be that.
> You should want this,
> you should want that.

Forcing their trauma onto you
without a second thought.

And what about the media?
here's a tea to make you pretty,
and here's the one to make you fit
and this one,
this one will make you sing
but,

> *my wrists are bleeding.*

"It's okay you look good, go find a man,"
and I search…

> I search within me
> but there's nothing there.
> I search within them

and that feels worse.

Emptiness,

I need someone to fill my cup with love,

with kindness,

with forgiveness.

Does anyone have a tea that could fill this void?

He smiles as he hands me

yet another shot

and I take it

because you see,

the only thing wrong

with feeling empty

is that you take whatever

you can get,

and when you have nothing to offer,

they only give you the worst of them.

What does rock bottom look like?

It looks like the fear

of wanting the negative to stop

and taking the easy route,

knowing you still have

so much more to give

and you surely haven't done enough.

It looks like the fear

you eat for breakfast

and wear around like clothes

so that men don't look and

feel entitled to comment

on the corners of your lips.

The fear that stops you from

standing where I am

the fear that tells you,

you are not good enough,

ENOUGH!

This is who I am.

These old scars?

They're just from a time

that I wasn't so strong.

These tears?
They come and go just like
everything else.
But him?
He might leave too
or he could stay
and if he does,
will you give your all?
Will you tell him about
the scars and the tears?

The tears that brought the scars,
the scars that brought the tears,

the fear

the fear

the fear

Will you let go of abandonment
that no longer pertains to you?

Because you are here
and so is he

and now tell me,

will you let him fill your cup?

Out of this World

I learned that I can trust you
on water and on land.

And if for some reason
we had to go to space,

I'd trust you there too.

Demons

When you argue with me
I feel loved.
When you are jealous
I feel wanted.

But don't forget
That when you are loving
I feel loved,
and when I am free
I still feel wanted.

Don't love me the way
my demons invite you to.
Love me the way you know best.

Road Trip

Five doors
and I chose to not run,
from myself
or from him
on an open road
where the places to go
are endless.

Do I want a mountain
or a lake big enough
to hold all of my sorrows?

Or do I want the van
that sometimes feels
like it's closing in?

But never tight enough
before it expands
and shows me
a sea of possibilities.

Choice

I chose him

from the moment our eyes met,

through misunderstandings

growth,

and change.

Through the times

we've felt far away

or close to falling apart,

I chose him.

Whether it's about

beige or green,

wood or ceramic,

cat or dog,

yes or no,

I already chose him.

June 20th

You woke me up
what I thought would be
the first out of many times.

There were only two.

You started out as
a bright light,
connecting my heart
to the rest of me
in a way
I've never loved myself like before.

It proved to me
that existence
of a god,
and of so much more.

It made what I wanted clear
and who I wanted it with
clearer.

It reminded me

that I can be better

and that I am perfect

as I am because you chose me.

July 18th

Am I awake,

or is this just a dream?

Either way,

I don't want it to stop.

I don't want you to stop

making your way to me.

I've told you a million times

even though I know

it's not up to you or me.

Our souls are so close together,

but not yet intertwined,

and as much as I want to

mold you into me

and protect you from

what I deep down begin to understand,

I know it's not up to you or me,

so I let go...

July 25th

I didn't need to
be woken up this time.
I laid in bed,
     pretending to sleep,
     pretending it wasn't happening.

I tried to hold myself together,
so tightly,
I almost exploded.

I wish I had
at least then I'd have an explanation
 I could accept,
for your absence
and for all the blood
that rushed out of me,
as if I had been holding
it against its will.

Dementia III

I now know
the importance
of a touch.

Even with our hands
covered in the remnants
of *Jabón de Cuaba*
and hand sanitizer,
they are also covered
with longing for one more.

One more kiss,
one more hug,
one more moment where
you'll remember me.

Whenever I call my dad

He asks me to bring him:

1. Prosciutto
2. Peanuts
3. Queso en hoja
4. Croissants
5. Pistacchios
6. Cookies
7. Empanadas
8. Chocolate
9. Hershey's Chocolate
10. Walnuts
11. Un sandwich de *Barra Payán*

I always show up.

Dementia IV

The irony of life,

I thought,

as I brushed clean my

father's dentures

at the nursing home

he's been living in

for over a year.

My mind flashed back

to when he used to take care

of my teeth.

If they were loose,

he would pull them.

If I was being stubborn,

he'd remind me of the importance

of brushing my teeth.

And here I was,

holding his smile in my hands.

Free

My grandfather revolted
against Trujillo.
I revolted against my parents,
who revolted against their beliefs,
and the tight grip of the trauma
that chained us all at our ankles.

Guns became words,
blood became tears
and victory became each one of us.
Standing up for what we are,
knowing what we want,
and what we don't.

Saying no
became a yes
that brought us closer
to our purpose
and we are free.

We are free
until we dictate otherwise
and only you,

and only me,

can place us behind the bars

that keep us away from

everything we've ever wanted.

English

I refused to speak English from the 7th grade through the 8th and most of High School whenever I could get away with it. The English language was reserved for very specific situations, and would exclusively be spoken to those that couldn't speak Spanish, or when prompted by teachers. My Spanish speaking friends knew that they could speak to me in English and that I would reply in Spanish.

It felt as if every time I tried to speak English something terribly embarrassing would happen, like the time my health teacher, tired of my lack of participation, asked me to read a paragraph out loud. I tried to refuse but she insisted that if I didn't read the paragraph, I would fail the class. An offer I would've gladly accepted had that been a choice.

The entire class stood silent while the teacher stood in front of my desk and insisted it was a "short" paragraph and that I should "just read it."

I gave in.

I decided to read very slowly to lower my chances of making a mistake. I landed on a word I had often heard before but could not remember how to pronounce. All I knew about the word was that it was not pronounced the way it looked. I took a long pause, hoping someone would rescue me by saying the word for me, the way the too-smart-for-their-own-good students like to do but no one did.

I braced myself for the mocking and read it slowly: *"Foh-ock You's,"* is what came out of my mouth.

"I'm sorry, what?" replied my teacher.
"Foh-ock You's?" I asked.

"Focus," finally said another student, *"She means focus."* Everybody erupted in laughter.

"Focus," I repeated quietly as I closed my book and sank into my seat.

As Long as I Speak

I've always been sensitive

but never more

than I am stubborn.

The day I heard the words

"Speak English, you're in America,"

I made a choice:

If I had to give up

one language for simply

existing in this foreign land,

it wasn't going to be

the one that taught me

everything I knew up to that point.

In Spanish,

I learned the difference

between me gustas,

te quiero

y te amo

and the importance

of each journey

as one travels from one to the other.

I learned the difference

111

Between *enamorarse*
y "tener un aficie del diablo"
and the importance
of volume,
when choosing between
¡Un coño y un coñazo!

In Spanish I learned,
that sometimes all you
need to communicate
is your body as you sing along
to a bachata,
feeling a heartbreak that isn't yours.

Trading my native language
For one that uses the word
"Cricket" exclusively
to describe the insect
and its pots only for cooking,
it's not an option.
I'll be damned
if I only speak English
just because
I am in America.

Dear Ms. Herrington

I know where I am.

I knew it back then too.
It's forever stamped
on my American passport.

What you didn't know
is that where I came from
is forever stamped inside of me.

Did you think I'd forget?
Did you think that
by silencing me,
I'd stop being from
somewhere else?
And all of a sudden
become an American
like you claim to be.

My big lips,
the same ones
you tried to silence,
my caramel skin,

the same one

you tried to break through,

and my wide hips,

the same ones

that shamefully

walked out of that room.

would have given me away.

Yeah, we are in America,

but I am Dominican and I

speak Spanish.

PORTAL

Toma, para que no te vayas a besar con un negro de alla: "Here so you don't go kissing any black guys over there." In this situation, negro was used referring to a black Dominican man, which really highlights the racism dark skin Dominicans face coming from light skin Dominicans.

Juana, Juana pelame la banana. Si no me la pelas, me la pela tu hermana: These are lyrics from a song

¿Tienen hambre? Are you hungry? Also known as the intro to most of the conversations in my family.

La salonera: The hair stylist. Back home, la salonera was a family friend who would show up around 9:00AM right on time for the morning coffee and didn't leave until 7:00PM after dinner. In that time, she would do everyone in my family's hair. The women would get their hair dyed, cut and styled, the men got haircuts and the kids would get blowouts and if we were lucky, we would get one highlight here and there.

Callejón: Alley. Mamá's apartment had one that went all the way around the back of the building. She had mango and cherry trees back there and we would climb the fire escape to reach the fruit and to talk to the workers from the restaurant next door.

Pan de Maíz: Corn bread. My abuela's specialty. Ever since I can remember, we'd go visit my grandma and she'd always have freshly baked pan de maíz. When we moved to America, she would come visit us and bake it for us at our home.

Heladero: Ice cream man, not truck. Back home, the ice cream man pushes around a cart, rings around a bell & yells *"Heladero!"*

Mis sueños no tienen lengua: My dreams have no tongue.

Voladora: Flying roach.

La Taza: The cup. When I was a child, I would watch all the adults sit around drinking their coffee and talking. After somebody was done, the person experienced in reading the cup would look inside and tell you your future.

La curiosidad mató al gato: Curiosity killed the cat. In my childhood, this was my mother's way of telling us to mind our business.

Tú ni te sabes lavar el culo bien: "You don't even know how to wash your behind properly," which means you haven't acquired basic life skills yet and this means you aren't not prepared to do the same things adults are allowed to do.

Por estar puteando te pasa: "That's what you get for slutting around." My parents were very strict especially when it came to boys and dating. If you did anything they didn't approve of, it was labeled slutting around.

Rama de limón: Lemon tree branch, Mama's weapon of choice when we weren't listening. It was the itchiest of the plants we kept around our apartment, and it did the job.

Jabón de Cuaba: is the soap in a Dominican household. When I was little, it was instilled in me that this was the only soap to shower with and for a few years after arriving in America, it was one of the things that made me feel closer to home. During the pandemic, I decided to buy Jabón de Cuaba, part because a part of me still believes it's a great disinfectant soap and part because it was a really anxiety ridden time and I needed to feel home again. During this time, I read the label and realized this soap is also used for washing clothes. I still feel cleaner when I use it to wash my hands.

Trujillo: A Dominican dictator who ruled the Dominican Republic from 1930-1961. My grandfather on my father's side was murdered in front of my grandmother, aunt, uncles, and father under Trujillo's ruling as they tried to escape by making their way into the Brazilian embassy. This is a delicate story that would take much more time and dedication to be told but it is important for me to mention here in a bit more detail because it was my grandfather's brave actions that set into motion what MANY years later would give me and my sisters the ability to obtain our American citizenship way faster than the average person.

117

Me gustas: I like you.

Te quiero: Lighter version of I love you.

Te amo: I love you.

> *Because of these last 3 words, I've always felt as if in my relationships, there's been levels, first there's a me gustas, then a te quiero and lastly, the final level is te amo as opposed to in English, where we go from Me gustas to Te amo. Thinking back as an adult, some of my relationships never went past te quiero, but because I was loving in English, I expressed them as a te amo and it blurred so many lines.

Enamorarse: To fall in love.

Tener un aficie del diablo: To be so in love, you can't breathe. "Aficie" is a shortened slang for "asfixiarse" which is to asphyxiate. The literal translation is the action of "having a goddamn asphyxiation."

Coño: There are many different meanings for this expression depending on what country it is being used but for me, it is closer related to a "Damn."

Coñazo: A bigger damn.

ACKNOWLEDGEMENTS

I am grateful to both my parents for making the difficult decision to leave our home and start over in the United States. To my dad, I know music, art and adventure because of you and to my mother, you taught me the importance of quick humor and finding even a hint of happiness in any situation.

My sisters, Natasha & Heidi, my sun & my moon, my light and my dark. Without both of you I simply wouldn't be. I've always felt protected by you despite the ocean that separates us. Because of you, I've never felt alone. To my sister Sandra, you showed up when it was important that you did, and I'll never forget that.

Michael, the adventurous man who leaves cabinet doors open: it matters not who swiped right first but that we'll continue to laugh and explore by each other's side. Your unconditional support pushed me to write my first 3 poems that night when I tried to self-sabotage my way out of it. Your leadership inspires me every day.

Lariannie & Giselle, you've lived almost every page of this book with me. No matter where we are in the world and in life, I am lucky to be endlessly held by strong women like you. No matter how much time goes by, we'll always be the three little teenagers, walking down our High School hallways, arms locked together and laughter all around.

Mckenna & Mallorie, you've been a part of the most important parts of my journey, through all phases, decisions, disappointments, and successes. We've laughed, we've cried, we've lived together and now really far apart and still, this sisterhood knows no bounds.

Thank you to the teachers that ever since I arrived in this country, ignited my passion for writing and the belief in endless possibilities: Mr. Bloom, Mr. Murphy, Professor Celia Reissig-Vasile & Professor Alan Hartman.

Coach Mary Touhey, my school mom & the best coach I could've dreamed of, High School would not have been the same without you. Your nurturing ways created a space that I looked forward to being in every single day of the week for four years.

Angy Abreu for founding the Dominican Writers Association, thanks for creating a platform and space for writers like me. Your devotion to seeing us grow is immeasurable. To the original Writer's Workshop, a group of the most inspiring and authentic writers I know especially Roxana Calderón, for not only editing this work with me once and then again, but making the process feel safe and familiar each time & Lisa Ventura for supporting me through this process, sharing the same journey and saying yes enthusiastically whenever you could.

Mi familia: Mamá, Abuela, Tia Maria, Guelo, Tia Kanka, Enmy, Riqui, Enrique, Magelline, Marlene, Osvaldo, Yorjan, Livi, James my cousin from Colorado and my abuelos whom I never met but whose stories have carried their love and legacy through all these years.

And to anyone else not mentioned by name but who has been or is a part of my life and this year-long process, and those whom I've had small interactions with that have led me to where I am today. I thank you deeply.

ABOUT THE AUTHOR

Carolina Abreu is a writer based in New York City. She was born in the Dominican Republic and moved to the United States in 2002. Her work has been displayed at *HBO's The Inspiration Room* (March 2019) and published in various publications: *LNNY Blog (November 2017 - April 2019), Palabritas (Mi Mamá, December 2019), Dominican Writers Association (The Piercing on my Face Makes me Ugly & Other Lies Told by my Culture/Donde Comen Uno Comen Dos, January 2020, April 2020) and The Ice Colony (Left Behind, October 2020).*

With her work, Carolina looks to create a space of vulnerability, self-love, liberation, and kindness; to inspire her generation and the future ones to believe in their authenticity while watering the roots planted by their ancestors. She believes in the importance of taking the strength of the past and the present and using it to create a new path that is paved with inclusivity, acceptance, and healing.

Speak English, You're in America is her first self-published poetry collection in which she explores what it means to belong, not just in the new country she was forced to begin calling home but in other aspects of life too. Her journey in the search for a sense of belonging takes us through her childhood, half in the Dominican Republic, half in the United States, her family life, trauma, relationships, self-discovery and lastly, the realization that she belongs wherever she chooses to stay.

CPSIA information can be obtained
at www.ICGtesting.com
Printed in the USA
BVHW031425300122
627213BV00003B/18